I0021511

Quantum computers, AI and humans

Who we are and what happened

Jin Schofield

Legal and Disclaimer

The information contained in this book and its contents is not designed to replace or take the place of any form of medical or professional advice; and is not meant to replace the need for independent medical, financial, legal or other professional advice or services, as may be required. The content and information in this book have been provided for educational and entertainment purposes only.

The content and information contained in this book have been compiled from sources deemed reliable, and it is accurate to the best of the Author's knowledge, information, and belief. However, the Author cannot guarantee its accuracy and validity and cannot be held liable for any errors and/or omissions. Further, changes are periodically made to this book as and when needed. Where appropriate and/or necessary, you must consult a professional (including but not limited to your doctor, attorney, financial advisor or such other professional advisor) before using any of the suggested remedies, techniques, or information in this book.

Upon using the contents and information contained in this book, you agree to hold harmless the Author from and against any damages, costs, and expenses, including any legal fees potentially resulting from the application of any of the information provided by this book. This disclaimer applies to any loss, damages or injury caused by the use and application, whether directly or indirectly, of any advice or information presented, whether for breach of contract, tort, negligence, personal injury, criminal intent, or under any other cause of action.

You agree to accept all risks of using the information presented inside this book. You agree that by continuing to read this book, where appropriate and/or necessary, you shall consult a professional (including but not limited to your doctor, attorney, or financial advisor or such other advisor as needed) before using any of the suggested remedies, techniques, or information in this book.

Table of Contents

Introduction

The human brain is one of the most complex machines we know of. In this book, we will discover how the brain developed and what its functions are. We will find out the parts that make it up and how it controls our everyday lives.

The complexity of the human brain has always challenged scientists and computer programmers the world over. They are trying to understand it better by creating something that will be intelligent with the use of non-biological materials—an artificial intelligence. We will look at its uses and how it compares to the human brain.

The concept of quantum computers has been around for quite a while now and they are slowly becoming a reality. These extremely powerful machines use principles at the subatomic level to make calculations at astonishing speeds. Some have compared the brain to a quantum computer. In this book, we will find out how they are alike and if the brain truly is a quantum computer.

Enjoy!

Humans and Our Brain

Humans are the most dominant species on the planet right now. With our numbers running up to above 7 billion, we have settled nearly every part of the world. What made human beings one of the most successful organisms on this planet? There is only one dominant answer: our brain.

The Development of Humans

Humans evolved from an ancestor that lived over 3 million years ago. As time progressed, this ancestor learned how to walk on two legs which made its forelimbs free to manipulate its environment. As our ancestors developed further, they learned how to use tools to hunt animals for food. After they controlled fire and learned to cook their food, the development of our early ancestors skyrocketed.

It is not true that humans descended from monkeys. That statement is completely false. What is true is that humans and modern-day apes and monkeys shared a common ancestor and thus developed alongside each other. This situation is somewhat analogous to a tree which only has one trunk but has a lot of different branches. After many evolutionary steps, we have arrived to the humans as we are today. But we didn't start out like this, though. There have been great developments in technology and society. These developments are truly groundbreaking and changed the ways that people lived. History is full of these discoveries and achievements, some of which we still use today albeit in an improved and better form or way. We owe a lot to the great men and women in history who worked hard not just to make their own lives better but that of those around them as well.

One of the times where technology truly exploded was in the 20th century. There have been great and amazing innovations and inventions during this time. Humans first discovered heavier than air flight during the early parts of the 20th century. It is also in this century that humans were able to harness the power of atoms. Almost all of the sectors of society benefited from these developments and society grew even more than before.

What powered these innovations and inventions? What tool this these great people use to make their plans and ideas come to life? The answer: their own brains.

The Human Brain

The human brain is one of the most important organs in our body. It controls every function of the body. Without it, you would be a useless pile of cells and body fluids. The brain never stopped working ever since it was "turned on". It works when we are awake and going about our daily lives and even when we sleep at night.

Evolution

The human brain is the main driving force between the development and growth of human beings. Its development is directly the reason why humans progressed the way we did. But how did it grow? What were the situations which made the brain grow and develop into what it is now?

The human brain was not what it is now. It used to be a lot similar to the brains of other primates. But, over the millennia that passed, something happened that changed the way the human brain looks and functions. One of the most notable differences is in the size of the brain's frontal cortex. This area of the brain is where most of the thinking done by humans is made. This is essentially where our intelligence originates. As time moved on, the size of the brain became larger and larger until it reached its present size. That is not the end of its development though. The brain may be large and the human can do some form of thought or formulate ideas, but there are still some differences between the brains of an early human to that of a modern one.

One of the most noticeable differences is the development of an area in the human brain that is solely dedicated to speech. This area is small or totally nonexistent on the brains of other primates, but since humans learned how to talk, this area of the brain has developed. The other area of the brain that differs from the brain of our ancient ancestors is an area called the neocortex. The neocortex is the newest part of the brain that developed. It is a brain area that is only found in mammals. This area of the brain is responsible for higher brain functions as the control of senses, intelligence, reasoning, and language. Scientists have found that the neocortex grows, or at least its folds and development increases, as the social structure of the individual widens or broadens. So, this means that the more social an individual is the more developed his neocortex may become.

How it works

The human brain is one of the parts of the human body that still contains some mysteries, up to this day.

There are things that are essential to humans that scientists have yet to find an area of the brain that it controls. One of these things that still remain unknown, or at least unexplained, is where human consciousness comes from. Scientists have mapped the entire brain but the root of consciousness is still to be found. But we're not here to talk about where consciousness comes from; we're here to get more information on how the brain works. So, let's get on with it.

The brain works using electrochemical signals that are passed to brain cells, or neurons, from other adjacent neurons. These tiny electrical impulses travel within the brain and to the specific part of the body that it controls. That is the way that messages or information from the brain is sent to the parts of the body.

This is also the same way that the environment interacts with the brain. The sensory organs, like the eyes, send signals to the brain on what they capture and the brain interprets those signals to form a coherent image. Think of it like this: There is a person inside a completely enclosed spaceship. This spaceship is traveling in space; there are no windows, the person inside cannot directly hear, feel, or smell what's going on outside. But the ship has sensors that send back the signals and the data they collect about the outside of the ship to the person. The brain functions the same way. It is like the person in the ship; the brain does not physically touch, see, or feel the outside world, but it uses the sensory organs to send information back to it.

Another function of the brain is to regulate the body. There are a lot of functions in the human body, something as basic as walking is controlled by the brain. We take walking for granted, most of the time, and it is an automatic function of the body.

We barely think of the way we walk. We normally just get the idea of going in one direction and just do it. What we don't see is how the brain controls it. But, before we go any further into how the brain works, let's first look at the parts of the human brain.

Major Parts of the Human Brain
Cerebrum

The cerebrum is the biggest part of the human brain and is responsible for most of the voluntary functions of it. This part of the brain is what controls reading, emotions, learning, speech, and movements that we think about. When someone says the word 'brain' this is usually the part that first comes to mind. The cerebrum contains a lot of folds and wrinkles and this is its most distinguishing feature. This part is made up of what are called grey and white matter.

The cerebrum is made up of two hemispheres, and each hemisphere has four sections or lobes. These lobes are called frontal, parietal, temporal and occipital. The frontal lobe is mostly responsible for reasoning and decision-making.

The parietal lobe is responsible for voluntary motion. The temporal lobe deals with the sounds and speech, it also is responsible for memories. Lastly, the occipital lobe is the part that deals with vision.

Cerebellum

The Cerebellum, or "Little Brain", is the part of the brain that is positioned below the cerebrum. It is like a smaller version of the cerebrum. Scientists have determined that this part of the brain is "older" than the cerebrum. How is it "older"? Scientists have found the same structure on more primitive animals like reptiles. This means that the cerebellum is, by the standards of evolution, much older than the cerebrum because even less developed animals have it.

The cerebellum is associated with regulation coordination of movement. Any damage to it may cause loss of fine motor control which means more erratic or unrefined voluntary movements. The cerebellum also plays a part in learning and other aspects controlled by the cerebrum, albeit at a much simpler or primitive way. The cerebrum and cerebellum together control the voluntary actions and motions of the human body.

Brain Stem

The Brain Stem is located directly below the center of the cerebrum and in front of the cerebellum. This part of the human brain controls the involuntary or automatic functions of the human brain. These functions are usually the most vital ones like breathing and keeping the heart beating. It is also responsible for the cycles that humans go through, like the sleeping cycles and the sensation of hunger. It also controls the sensation of pain.

The brain stem is also the pathway for all signals coming from and into the cerebrum. Any damage to the brain stem is usually fatal and very serious.

How the Brain Functions

Now that we have tackled the main parts of the human brain, let us now delve deeper into how it really works. As said before, the signals to and from the brain travel through neurons. These neurons pass the signal to the next one until it reaches the brain or the organ it is attached to. Now, let's see how one movement is performed. Let's pick a simple one, like lifting a pen.

One of the first things that happen is the cerebrum fires up and decides that it wants to pick up a pen. What it will do then is to scan the memories of what a pen looks like. This may not seem too obvious but, the decision making part of the brain is not the same part that holds memories, so these parts communicate with one another. Once the appropriate information about the item is received, the signal is passed on to the eyes in order to look for that item. The eye then sends a signal that the item has been found. The brain then sends a signal to the arm, via the brain stem, to extend the muscles of the arm, hand, and fingers to pick up the pen. The nerves at the fingers then report that the pen is in the hand and it gives the signal.

Now, do you see how a seemingly simple process that we don't even notice takes a lot of steps to be performed? Doing this step-by-step process seems to take a lot of time, but in actual practice, this whole process barely takes a second. The brain does this while still keeping all the other parts of the body running.

So, as you can see, the human brain is a very complicated machine. It controls a lot of functions and responsibilities that are vital to human life. In a way, the brain is directly responsible for all the achievements and technological advances we have. It holds who and what we are. And it also holds the ways in which we can achieve a better and brighter future.

Artificial Intelligence

Technology has been part of human development since the beginning. Ever since the early humans picked up rocks and sticks to use them as tools for hunting, the technology we have has steadily improved. The things that we take for granted today will astound anyone from the past if they were brought to our time. Imagine someone like Albert Einstein, arguably one of the best minds that ever existed, being stumped and unable to use a computer or a smart phone. Imagine someone from an earlier time period, like Sir Isaac Newton, being spooked by an airplane or a car.

Artificial Intelligence defined

Humans have always wanted to improve their own lives, and by extension, that of those around them. This leads to a lot of discoveries and inventions that changed the world.

When humans needed a faster way of transportation that does not use their feet, they tamed animals that they can ride on. Most chose horses, while others, especially in the Middle East, chose camels and other types of animals.

Improvements have been invented to improve this form of transport. The taught the animals to pull something that they can ride on. But this still did not stop the development. Other, faster modes of transport were invented like the train and the car. Up to this day, improvements are always being made to the things that humans already have.

One recent invention that constantly gets better is the computer. The computer revolutionized the way humans lived. Ever since it was first invented it changed lives. Now computers that are multiple times more powerful than the early ones are in almost everyone's pocket. What runs these computers have evolved as well.

A program is a set of instructions that tell a computer what it can and cannot do. It also dictates how the computer will perform a certain action. This can be as simple as displaying a word on the screen or something that works entirely in the background. As the years go by, the programs have become more and more complicated. They started from holes in a card that represent the ones and zeros that the computer understands. Now, there are a lot of programming languages that can be used to program a computer.

One of the programs that humans have been tinkering with is called Artificial Intelligence. This program's goal is to make the computer 'think' like a human. These machines are able to do what a human can do if he were in the same situation. At least that's the goal. A fully complete Artificial Intelligence, or AI, machine has never been developed—yet.

Advancements in computer technology have made the AI's we already have more powerful and useful. AI is currently being used in a lot of aspects of life like medicine, transportation, communications and many more. As the programs and computers are getting more advanced, so too will the uses of AI. There may come a time when AI runs our daily lives. Whether that day will come or if it will be favorable for us is a question that still has no definite answer. But one thing is for sure, AI is already here and it will only develop further.

Types of AI

There are a lot of examples of AI in our everyday lives. Later, we'll check out the uses of them, but for now, let's first look at the different types of AI, whether it already exists or not.

Weak AI

Weak AI is currently the only types of AI program that we have. These are AI programs that mainly do just one task automatically. It is also called Narrow AI because of the narrow tasks that it can perform. It solves a very specific problem that may use pre-defined responses to certain questions. It may have some form of speech recognition but it is not that accurate—it may still miss some things. Narrow AI is also used for repetitive work which ensures that the items or products that it makes are identical in every way. This form of AI is the most widely spread. It is being used for factories, economics, and communication. Weak, or Narrow, AI can also be used as an educational tool.

Strong AI

Artificial General Intelligence, or AGI, is the main goal of those who are working on this program. It is more commonly called Strong AI or Full AI. This form of Artificial Intelligence is considered to be truly intelligent. It has all the functions of a human brain, especially in problem solving and reasoning. It also has the ability to learn from its past experiences. Another aspect of this type of AI is its ability to develop consciousness. So, essentially, the person who creates this will only have to enter the basic information he thinks the AI will need and the capacity to do those functions, and the program will figure out everything else on its own. This is the type of AI mostly shown in movies and science fiction.

The search for AGI is still ongoing and may yield some results in the future. The development of AGI can potentially solve a lot of problems but may also create others. These will be discussed later in the chapter. But, what we have right now are tests for Artificial Intelligence programs to determine their "intelligence". One of the most common forms of a test is called the Turing Test.

The Turing Test, developed by programmer Alan Turing in the 1950's, is a way to gauge if a program has "intelligence". This is how it works. A human and a computer are conversing with a person. None of them can see one another. The person asks a series of questions to both the human and the computer. If the person, or evaluator, cannot tell the difference between the two, the computer passes the test.

This is just one of the many forms of tests that can gauge if an AI program has "intelligence".

But for now, we still do not have this form of AI. Whether it will be beneficial or not, depends on many factors.

Superintelligence

The next step above the AGI is called superintelligence. This form of AI surpasses the intelligence of any human being on the planet. It learns and improves on its own without the help of humans or other computers. This is the ultimate form of AI that we currently think of. Superintelligence does not limit itself to computers though. Research and future studies show the possibility of having a biological superintelligence. This means that the human brain is combined or augmented with AGI and improves his intellectual abilities.

This form of AI is still being widely debated whether it is feasible or not, and, if it is possible, how will it change the lives of humans around the globe.

The Uses of AI

Artificial Intelligence, or at least a Weak AI, is currently being used in the entire world. Here are just some examples of the current uses of AI in different facets of society.

Medical

Artificial Intelligence programs are currently being used in medicine to help doctors in diagnosing their patients. AI also helps in the "electronic health records" of patients. Robots with AI programs are also being used in performing surgeries. AI also helps in the creation and development of drugs and treatment plans for many kinds of illnesses and diseases.

Transportation

Transportation is one of the industries that have been greatly improved by AI programs. From the production of cars to the way the car works are helped or improved upon by AI. Manufacturing the cars and the parts that make it up are being assisted by AI robots.

By far the most obvious application of AI in transportation is the development of driverless vehicles. These cars can safely transport passengers and cargo without the aid of a human. They scan the route and their surroundings to make decisions in transporting their load. Traffic and congestion can also be improved by the widespread use of autonomous vehicles that communicate with one another. It is also a way to avoid road-related accidents.

Business and Economics

AI is also widely used in the business world. It has been used in a lot of business and investment related decisions. It is also used to help answer the questions of customers through the use of "chatbots". Artificial Intelligence systems also use algorithms to determine when and where to place advertisements. This maximizes the profitability of a certain business by targeting specific audiences for the ad AI is also being used to help people and investors with their finances. It uses the data to create algorithms to determine how to invest the money for maximum profit.

Video games

A lot of video games use the term AI loosely. But there is a form of AI that mimics the way a human plays the game. This is most commonly applied in FPS (First-Person-Shooting) and MMORPG (Massively Multiplayer Online Role Playing Game) games. Programmers have developed an AI program that learns from the playing style of human players and mimics or improves upon them. AI programs have also been used to "cheat" on some games.

Military

Unmanned vehicles have been used in the military for a while now. There are a lot of planes, like the Predator Drone, that does not have a physical pilot in its cockpit. Instead, the plane is being remotely controlled by a pilot from a safe location. AI in the military removes the human component of this equation completely. Development of autonomous ships, submarines, and tanks are being performed by some of the most technologically advanced nations. Another possible use of AI in the military is the artificial soldier or combatant. Instead of having human soldiers on the battlefield risking their lives, robots and autonomous vehicles can be used to minimize casualties.

Construction & Manufacturing

Planning and designing a building takes a lot of calculations to ensure the safety and integrity of a structure. AI is being used to quickly make plans and calculations to make the job of engineers and architects easier. Autonomous construction vehicles and equipment are also being developed. This not only optimizes the work but also improves the safety of the site. In terms of manufacturing and production of goods, AI is being widely used. It is mainly applied to robots. These robots perform tasks that are impossible or hazardous to humans. Robotic arms also perform repetitive and intricate tasks during the manufacturing of a product. This reduces error in production and removes the risk of accidents.

The Future of AI

The rapid development and improvement of AI programs will definitely have an effect on the way people live.

As said earlier, these changes can be good or bad for us—or they can be both. Whatever the case may be, Artificial Intelligence is being developed further, and will probably stay with us. So, let's examine the way Artificial Intelligence is going to affect human lives in the future, especially if these AI programs have the same "intelligence" as humans. There are a few questions that remain to be answered though. Is the development of AI, more specifically AGI, ethical? How will a computer program view us? Will it have consciousness? How will a person control it? There are some questions that will be answered in this section. A lot of people, especially those who have been following science news, are excited about the development of more advanced AI. Right now, what is currently available on the market shows the advantages and some possible disadvantages of AI systems. Even though the current data shows that AI is positive, there are some people who are afraid of what the development of human-like, or near-human, artificial intelligence will bring. Will it improve the way people live? A lot of research shows that AI has a lot of advantages that improve the way humans live. But, the fear of more advanced AI cannot be just thrown away. These are potential issues that the developers of AI will have to solve before they happen. Providing assurance to the world that AI is safe will ensure that it becomes widespread and completely beneficial for humans.

Now, let's look at some optimistic and pessimistic view about AI and what it can do.

The Optimistic View

The development of AI will bring about, as future studies hope, a better and brighter future for humans and their daily lives.

The improvement of the daily routine is one of the goals of AI developers. They really want to make humans do things faster, safer, and more efficiently. The AI programs that we currently have are proof of that. Autonomous vehicles, robots, and digital financial advisers are just some of the examples of how AI is already improving the lives of people all around the globe.

But these are the benefits that we enjoy today. What about the future? As was shown earlier, there are a lot of uses for AI. But its usefulness does not end there. As AI systems get more and more advanced, they will impact a lot of things that will benefit us in the long run. Let's get into some details about those things.

One of the biggest things that will be changed if AI becomes more widespread and advanced is the transportation industry. Not only will self-driving cars be common, but they'll also probably be the main mode of transport for everyone. Some have likened these self-driving cars to the human body's red blood cells. As the cells travel throughout the human body, they are moving independently from one another. They get to their destination without any mishaps or accidents, no matter how narrow the blood vessels may be. This thought is being applied to autonomous vehicles most especially in terms of safety. Worldwide, millions of people are killed or injured from road-related incidents every year. With the introduction of self-driving vehicles, this will be greatly reduced as the cars are totally aware of their surroundings and can react to them much quicker than a human driver can. If a single network controls all of the cars on the road, they can communicate with one another and can adjust their route, speed, and direction according to what's around them.

Not only will this make traffic flow smoother, but it will also greatly improve road safety.

Another advantage that more advanced AI brings to the table is also related to safety. This time, though, it is directly related to humans. AI, or more specifically robots, does not feel pain. Moreover, they can be repaired if they are broken or destroyed. So, what this means is that they can take over the more dangerous jobs that humans are currently doing. Mining, welding, operating heavy equipment, and working at nuclear reactors are just some of the dangerous jobs that humans currently do. With the advancement of AI robots, these jobs, or at least the dangerous parts of these jobs, will be done by robots that are far easier to replace and less valuable than human lives. This does not mean that a human will be completely out of the picture.

A human may still be assigned to oversee the robots while they are doing their jobs. Another dangerous job that robots can do has something to do with the police force. Robots can be used to diffuse bombs or neutralize threats to the human population. Robots can also be used to explore space or the ocean. Because of the harsh conditions in these places, humans cannot directly go to them and explore. With robots and AI, they can be sent as probes or as first settlers to pave the way for humans and make the environment livable for them, especially on other planets. Not only can AI be used for dangerous jobs, but they can also be used for dull or tedious work. An AI does not need breaks or vacations, and it can do one small or big, job all on its own. AI robots may also be used as soldiers or police officers. No amount of money can ever pay for a human life, so robots can be used instead of people in fighting the enemy.

AI, or at least some parts of it, can be combined directly with a person in order to improve that person's abilities. This is called augmentation. Humans can add things to the body, permanently, that will improve their brain power or their physical strength. This technology can also be used for prosthetics and medicine. If a certain part of the body needs to be replaced, an autonomous part can be made so that it still feels and moves like the original part. Almost every person has a smartphone these days. But what if in the future we won't need physical phones anymore? What if the phone is already inside of you? You'll just have to think about calling someone, and you can talk to them directly without doing any physical activities. Sounds like science fiction, doesn't it? Well, for now, it still is. But in the future, as more advanced and better AI comes into the society, this might be the future that we have. The strength of the body can also be greatly improved. With augmentation, humans can become faster, stronger, and more intelligent than we have ever been.

One of the biggest problems that humans face right now is climate change. Along with the increase in the world's temperature, a lot of hurricanes and typhoons ravage multiple countries. There has also been an increase in drought and diseases. With the improvement and advancement of AI, they can be used to combat and solve these problems. AI and more advanced computations can help predict any natural disaster that may occur. This will help improve the response time to these situations which will save a lot of lives. More advanced AI can also improve the general well-being of every person. For example, superintelligence may be able to calculate how to disseminate the resources that the world has, which can make sure that no one will become hungry. War and famine may also become obsolete because of AI development since most wars are fought because of resources. AI, if used in robots, will create an artificial companion or a friend. They can also function as servants for people. This will greatly help those in need of personal care and attention. What this means is that hospitals and elderly care facilities do not have to employ a lot of people to take care of their patients. Another great advantage is that these robots do not get tired or take breaks. Robots can work 24 hours per day, and also seven days per week. This is great for hospitals and ICU's that take care of a lot of patients at the same time. Robots can also become companions for those who need them, especially those with mental health issues. Having someone to talk to who understands and knows what they're going through may greatly help with their treatment.

The Pessimistic View

While there are definitely a lot of benefits for the development of advanced AI, there are also some risks involved. Humans are generally accepting of change. It is what makes us thrive. The ability of humans to adapt to the environment is what made us the dominant species on the planet. But we have not yet encountered something that may completely change the way we live and survive so drastically. Most of the changes that occur in human history are slow and the effects are felt maybe a generation or two after its development. With the advancements in AI and the computer technologies, the pace at which developments happen has grown exponentially and the effects of developments and inventions are being felt by people within the same generation.

So, with the development and advancement of more and more sophisticated AI systems, how will this affect the lives of humans? Will it always be good? Will we finally live in a utopia? While some future studies show the great benefits of advanced AI technology, there are some very serious risks involved. Let's check them out in detail.

AI and robots can do a lot of jobs, as stated previously. Right now, they are only doing simple and basic jobs that are tedious or dangerous for humans to do. But what if, in the future, if AI systems have become even more sophisticated, they can do **everything** that a human can do and do it better? How will this affect our lives? This is a very real situation that is already happening, albeit on a smaller scale. Remember the robots that are doing the small, tedious jobs right now? Those things were done by a person before. A person who has a family to feed, children to send to school, and bills to pay. So now that a robot can do his job better and faster than he can ever do, he has been laid off from work. This is a situation that is happening all around the globe. Workers, especially unskilled ones, are being replaced by machines that can do their jobs. This is beneficial to the owner of the company that employs them as he will not have to pay salaries to a person; he'll only have to pay for the whole machine and maybe some maintenance, which is far cheaper than employing a person. But how will that change affect the person who has been laid off? A situation like this not only affects the employee but also those that depend on him. Right now, only small and simple jobs are being replaced, but what if all the jobs are being done by computers, AI systems, and robots, what will humans are doing? Will we become totally dependent on robots and computers for our daily lives?

But robots are not only going to take over small jobs. As they become more and more sophisticated, they can replace skilled workers and even professionals. This situation is called **technological unemployment**. Technological employment is the situation where humans are replaced by machines in their jobs. This often leads to poverty for the unemployed people. This is one scenario that some researchers fear because of the advancement of AI technologies.

Another scenario which stems from more advanced AI systems is the annihilation or subjugation of the human race by these systems. We all know that humans are the most advanced species on the planet. We have tamed the world and used it to improve ourselves. We have used, and are still currently using, the natural resources that Nature provides. We have controlled most animals that we know, even the wild ones like lions and tigers. Some have even become pets or food for us. But what if humans are replaced by AI systems as the dominant intelligence on the planet? What then becomes of us? Will we become slaves to these computers? Or will they completely destroy the human race? These are just some questions that AI programmers and researchers are trying to answer. They are looking for ways to control an AI program even if it becomes more intelligent than the smartest person that ever lived.

A scenario that some researchers fear is not that the AI develops consciousness and decides to destroy the human race. Instead, what they fear is that its goals may not be the same as the person who created it. As the AI systems get more and more intelligent, it may develop its own goals that have nothing to do with its original goal. Another, connected fear is that the goals of the creator and the AI system may be aligned, but the means in which the AI achieves its goal may be destructive. It may rush headlong into pursuing its programmed goal without checking on how its actions are affecting the world. In these scenarios, total control for the AI is necessary.

One of the more realistic risks for advanced AI systems is that they may be used for a destructive purpose. The terrorists and even powerful governments, when they get their hands on a powerful weapon, they will find ways to use it against their enemies. So, what is going to stop them from "weaponizing" an advanced AI program to do the dirty work for them? For example, a terrorist group might set off a bomb in a populated area without risking one of their own people. They could just send an automated car to a specific destination. They may even be able to get inside the networks of their target and steal confidential documents from them. Countries and nations may use advanced AI to target their own citizens in order to stay in power. These situations are currently happening without the aid of AI systems. Imagine how dangerous it will be if an AI programming is helping them do it. Nowhere will be safe from them.

Humans and AI

From a BBC interview, on December 2014 physicist Dr. Stephen Hawking said that "The development of full artificial intelligence could spell the end of the human race....It would take off on its own, and re-design itself at an ever-increasing rate. Humans, who are limited by slow biological evolution, couldn't compete and would be superseded." This is one of the fears that most humans have about AI technology is better and better with every iteration of it. So, let's look into the details as to how AI technology will bring about significant change in human lives. Let's check if these changes will be good or bad for us.

Human Workers VS AI Workers

The development of the modern automobile has changed a lot in the lives of horses. Horses used to be the main mode of transport for everyone. They were used in cities as a means of going around, they were used to move cargo and merchandise through great distances, they were used in farms and mines, and they were even used for warfare. But with the introduction of the automobile changed everything.

The horses were replaced with automobiles, even if the early automobiles were slower than the horses. The advantage of automobiles over horses stems from economics. The cost of having a horse and maintaining it is vastly more expensive than the maintenance of automobiles. They also brought more power at a lesser cost. A single automobile may have the same power as four or five horses. The automobiles did not need to be vastly better than the horse; it only had to do the same job as good as the horse, at just a lesser cost.

This phenomenon has happened in the past and is bound to happen again. The same way that horses were replaced by the automobile, humans are being replaced by robots and automated machines in their work. This does not only apply to the jobs in a factory, but this also applies to professionals. A lot of factory workers were replaced by automated machines that did their jobs the same way they did. The robots, or machines, did not need to be faster or better than the humans. They may have the same capabilities. What sets the machines apart, which incidentally made them more economically viable than humans, is that the machines never get tired. They can run for years with minimum maintenance. Whereas a human worker needs a break for food and rest every day. This brought a great advantage to the machines that led to them replacing humans in factories and production lines. Of course, there are still humans that work on these machines, but the number of people working on a single factory has been reduced from hundreds to just tens of people working on the whole line.

As robots, machines, and computer programs are getting better and better, they are bound to replace more and more humans in more and more jobs as time progresses.

The improvement of automated vehicles is already shepherding this revolution. The transportation industry employs a lot of people worldwide—at least 70 million people according to some estimates. The automated vehicle may replace these drivers just because they are more economically viable. A self-driving truck has a lot of advantages over a human driver. A human driver can be sleepy, tired, may become distracted, and needs to rest once in a while. An automated truck does not. Even something as small as a bathroom break affects the productivity of a worker. So, as computers develop, more and more people will become unemployed, not because they are lazy or do not fit the requirements for the job, they just aren't needed anymore. In the future, there may be signs that say that "Humans Do Not Need to Apply".

But white-collar jobs are not the only ones that may be replaced. Even professionals may become unviable, or no longer needed, for the jobs that they provide. Right now, there is a program called Watson that provides a medical diagnosis to a lot of patients accurately. This program delivers diagnoses based on a lot of factors and variables that human professionals cannot match. Even the job lawyers, or at least their paper works, may be done by computers. As these computers do not need to rest, sleep, eat, or drink, they are already more economically advantageous than their human counterparts. Coupled with the fact that these computers can go through thousands of documents in a matter of hours, compared to weeks for a human, already makes them better. What this shows is that the past is repeating itself. As more advanced computer programs and AI software are being developed, more and more jobs will become obsolete for humans.

But not all hope is lost though. There is, of course, still some skepticism about the fact that humans will become replaced by robots and computers. And there are still some jobs, or vocations, that robots and computers cannot do. But that list is getting smaller by the minute. So, what can we do about it?

One thing that is being done is to find ways to control the explosion and influx of computers in the workplaces of humans. Companies are still finding ways to employ people for different jobs. Programmers are also finding ways in order for people not to lose control over AI programs and systems. With the current trend of computer programming technology, humans are having less control over the development of AI programs. There is the concept of machine learning which means that the computer is learning on its own based on the data that is being given or fed to it. But that is where humans will still remain in control—the amount and kind of data that is being put into the system. There are programmers that make AI systems where input from humans is still needed. For example, an AI program called AIVA can compose music that is pleasing to the ears and seems to have been created by humans because its creators gave it the input that it needs in order to do so. So, in a way, even if AI programs become more and more advanced, there is still a human on the loop. This person's job may be as simple as pulling a plug or pushing a button when he feels that something is going wrong. Some AI skeptics are even supposing that every AI system still needs a human in the loop in order to feed data and information into it. So, some people are less worried about AI systems replacing them in their work. But we must still face the fact that, maybe one day, humans no longer need to work because an AI program is doing the work for them. Whether this will be good or bad is not certain. What we do know is that there is a possibility that this is where the future is headed.

The Brain VS AI Brains

An AI program is essentially just a simulation of the human brain. It tries to do what the human brain is currently able to do. And this is what current AI programmers aim to do. They want to create an AI system that works like the human brain. We all know that the human brain is a very complex machine—it is the most complex machine that we know—but it still is a machine. Its functions, its parts, and the function of those individual parts are being studied right now. There are some functions that we already know how it works. The challenge comes into applying it into an input that computers or AI systems understand. This is way harder than it sounds. As was shown earlier in this book, something as simple as picking a pen up involves a lot of steps and decisions that the human brain performs almost instantaneously.

People have been comparing the human brain and the computer for a long time. Of course, there are some tasks that AI programs and computers are better than a human, but the human brain outperforms AI programs over more general tasks and decision-making skills. Right now, most AI programs are only able to do simple tasks but as time goes by and technology improves, even more, they are catching up to humans quicker. A few of decades ago, computers are huge machines that are as large as a room. Now, there is a computer inside everyone's pocket. This is the trend that technology seems to follow. Technology is being used in order to develop better and better technology.

So, a general purpose AI might not be plausible in the coming decades but they may be available in the next century. Who knows?

But let's get into the comparison between a human brain and an AI that aims to replicate it. There are a few criteria where humans and AI programs can be compared against one another. These are Energy efficiency, processing power, universal use, and multi-tasking. So, let's get into more of these details.

Energy Efficiency

The human brain is a very powerful machine, as we have established earlier. What most people don't know is how energy efficient it is. The human brain only uses around 25 watts of energy to function, while machines that are only close to replicating a human brain already consume around 2000 watts of energy. This makes the human brain a lot more compact and has more function, even if it uses up a lot less energy than its digital counterpart. This is one of the key areas where the human brain vastly outperforms an AI system. And, you must remember, the AI systems we have, even the most advanced ones, are nowhere near replicating the human brain. So, a general purpose AI that functions the same way as a human brain does may need a lot more energy than the ones that we already have.

Processing Power

The biggest advantage of AI systems over human brains is the sheer power and amount of data a computer can process. We all know that a computer can outstrip a human brain in terms of processing power.

An AI system can take in millions of data at the same time and will process them faster and more accurately than a human can. This is one of the main reasons why AI programs are being developed. The amount of data that we currently have has grown ever since the advent of computers. The Internet also revolutionized the way that data is transferred. Another thing that gives AI systems an edge over human brains is that these AI systems do not get tired and can function 24 hours a day for seven days a week. Whereas a human needs to rest every few hours in order to function and work properly, an AI system does not. It is also vastly more accurate than any human. Since it processes a lot of data at the same time, it can make correlations and deductions based on the information it has. This reduces the amount of error to an almost negligible amount. The accuracy of these systems also makes them better than humans at sorting and categorizing things. And, as icing on the cake, an AI system can be used to replace a human on menial and boring tasks like going over paperwork and inventories.

Universal Use

As we have already established, the human brain remains to be the benchmark at which AI systems are being compared to. The human brain is very universal in its functions. It can do everything that it needs to do without having to rely on another machine or brain to do so. If there is something that a human does not know, he will still be able to learn it, given a short amount of time. AI systems, meanwhile, are currently only able to do a single task at a time. Even the most advanced AI systems are nowhere near the capabilities of the human brain. And the learning process for humans may only take a few hours or days in order for them to learn a new thing.

On the other hand, AI systems need a few weeks or even months before they can perform even a single task. The reason for this? The functions of the human brain may be known, but it is difficult to program an input for that specific function that a computer or an AI system understands. This is the current limitation that AI systems, or any computer program for that matter, have. A human brain is still needed in order for an artificial brain to function. The input and data that an AI system needs are still being fed into it by a person. Sure, it can learn from its previous calculations, but that will take a long time to process.

Multi-Tasking

There are advanced AI systems that are better than humans at certain, brain-related tasks like playing chess— where a computer program has beaten world chess champions—but that computer can only do one thing, play chess. It has become so good that it can beat the best human in chess because of the amount of information that it has. The computer can calculate all the possible moves in a chess game, but that is all it can do. While the person who was beaten by a computer can still do a lot of tasks without requiring another brain to do it for him.

This is another area where a human brain outshines an artificial one. The human brain can perform a variety of tasks at the same time. For example, a student is taking a test. The brain uses its processing power to recall all the lessons that it has learned. It then correlates that knowledge to the questions that need to be answered. If calculations are required for the question, the brain also recalls how that calculation progresses. Then it has to relay that information to the hand that does the writing for that test.

The brain functions as it does while still keeping the automatic body functions going. It has to regulate the breathing and movement of the lungs, the beating of the heart, and it also processes the inputs from all the senses. But that is not the only example of multi-tasking that a human brain does. Within a person's lifetime, the brain does a lot of functions and processes at the same time. The brain can be used to create works of art while still thinking about something you did a few hours ago. You can drive properly and follow all the rules of the road while talking to the person beside you. An AI system, or at least most of the ones that we have now, are still only able to do single tasks. But as technology improves, the AI system will become more and more complex. There are some systems that are able to do a couple of tasks at the same time. This will only improve in the years and decades to come, so an AI program that multi-task efficiently may just be a few years or decades away.

The Verdict

Human brains and AI systems have a lot of similarities and differences, as we have shown. There are some cases where an AI system is far better than a human brain, but there are also some areas where the brain is better. What this shows is that AI systems still have a long way to go before it can compare to the human brain for all its functions. But that future may come sooner than we think. Because the trend of technological development grows exponentially, it may take less for AI systems to be comparable to the human brain. As of right now, more advanced and more powerful AI systems are being developed and created. These systems can, in turn, be used to create other AI systems that are better than they are. So, even if the human brain has an advantage over AI systems right now, it may not
have it for long.

But of course, we also have to think of the risks involved in the development of these advanced systems. The risks and pessimistic views shown earlier are very real. We have seen human workers being replaced by mechanical workers that are more efficient than they are. So, we must be certain of how the development of AI will affect the world. It may be good at the beginning and improve a lot of lives, but, as history shows, what is good for one person may not be good for another. The introduction of automated machines in factories meant that a lot of low-skilled workers lost their jobs because a machine can do the same job for less. This will not only impact that person's life but also the lives of those around him. And on a larger scale, the unemployment will affect a country's economy greatly. We must safeguard ourselves in order for humans to still be in the loop on the creation and development of more advanced AI systems.

We must also make sure that these systems don't fall into the wrong hands. Even a concept that is designed for good may be used to do bad things if it were given to the wrong person. The development of advanced computer programs and AI systems will be wanted by a lot of people, both good and bad. So, in the name of the human race's safety and security, these programs must be kept secure.

Quantum Computers

Computers have revolutionized the way we have lived ever since they were introduced. They have also become more powerful over the years. Not only are the computers we have now so much more powerful than the ones before, but they are also a lot more compact. Old computers used to take up a lot of space—even a whole room—for just one machine. Now, everyone who has a smartphone has an extremely powerful computer in his or her pocket. Of course, as time progresses technology grows more complex and more powerful. This not just applies to computers but to every form of technology we have. An improvement for every form of technology that has been invented is normal. Not because something works, does not mean that it can no longer be improved upon. When it applies to computers, not only are the individual parts and components getting better and smaller, so too does the computer itself. The idea of a quantum computer has been thought about for quite a while now. The quantum computer is supposed to be a lot of times faster and more powerful than the fastest supercomputer we currently have.

What is a Quantum Computer?

"What precisely is a quantum computer?" A quantum computer is a device that uses phenomena based on quantum physics. In order to fully understand what a quantum computer is, we will first need to differentiate it from a conventional computer.

Conventional Computer VS Quantum Computer

Now, let's check out the differences between a quantum computer and a conventional one.

The thing that is totally different between the two is in the way that the data is encoded. This is the essentially the language in which the computer speaks. A conventional computer uses electronic signals that convert information into ones and zeroes, or more commonly known as bits, which it then uses for its calculations. A quantum computer uses superposition for calculations and storage of information which means it can store more information than a conventional one. But what is "superposition"? It is a concept in quantum mechanics that states two different quantum states can be combined together, or superposed, and combines into another valid quantum state. To put it simply, at any one time, a particle, for example, an electron can be in two places at the same time. The catch is this; its position becomes fixed once it is observed. If you have ever heard of Schrödinger's Cat, that is one of the simplest ways to explain superposition. As was said earlier, a quantum computer uses superposition to encode and calculate the data it has. A conventional computer uses 1's and 0's to encode its data and those positions are the only two possible states of that information. It is possible for the positions to be switched, but the bit can only have one value at a single time. The computer then reads those bits as its instructions for its functions and calculations. A quantum computer's data, meanwhile, can be a one, a zero, or both. This fundamental change allows the quantum computer to store more data with the same amount of storage space. These units are called quantum bits or qubits.

Advantages of a Quantum Computer

A quantum computer is seen as the next step in the development of computers. They are theoretically more powerful and faster than the computers we have now.

Using concepts of quantum physics and quantum mechanics, it is able to make more calculations and store more data. But what makes a quantum computer so much faster than a conventional one? As said before, a quantum computer uses qubits which can be in any or both states, as a one or a zero. This 'superposition' allows the quantum computer to make more calculations than a conventional one. But how does it do it? It's like this, for every question or problem you put on a quantum computer, multiple operations are already going on that calculate all the possible solutions to that problem. With multiple repetitions, it then churns out the correct answer to the problem or question being asked. It uses the quantum states and concepts and principles in quantum mechanics for these calculations. This phenomenon allows the quantum computer to perform calculations and computations much faster than a conventional computer can.

Another concept of quantum mechanics that allows quantum computers to have more processing speed and power is the concept of 'entanglement'. This concept says that if you measure quantum states or particles that are entangled, you only need to measure one of the states or particles and you will also get information about the other particles or states entangled to it. This effect does not depend on the distance of the particles or states. Albert Einstein once called this phenomenon, "spooky action at a distance".

How Does It Work?

A quantum computer uses the superposition and entanglement of quantum states and particles to perform calculations that a conventional computer cannot. Or, if the calculation is something a regular computer can do, the quantum computer will do it faster. But how does it work?

In order for us to understand the way a quantum computer works; we'll first have to know how a regular computer works. As previously stated, a conventional computer converts the data it receives into a series of ones and zeroes. It then uses these bits as instructions and information for the calculations it will perform. Let's use an example. Let's say there are eight people who want to enter a club. Each person is assigned a series of ones and zeroes. For this example, we will be using three digits so that each person will have a unique number. Each person with the number 1 will be able to enter, even if there is just a single one in their three-digit number. They are all trying to pass a security officer at the door. If the officer is in a good mood, he will allow all of them to enter. If he's not, he will only allow half of them to get in. Here is where the separation between conventional computers and quantum computers happen. A conventional computer will look at every single person's number. The minimum number of times the computer will look for that number is five. A quantum computer will only have to calculate once. But there's a catch. Because of the nature of quantum mechanics, if a particle in superposition is observed or measured, it will break down. So, if a qubit in superposition is observed, it will break down into a one or a zero but it cannot be both at the same time. So, the output of the quantum computer is another quantum state where the individual values for each qubit cannot be known but only the 'relationship' between them.

So, for our example, the quantum computer will not show you the numbers that each of the eight people has. Instead, the quantum computer will tell you the security officer's mood. With this information, you will know the correlation within the people in the group based on the mood of the security officer.

The (Potential) Uses of Quantum Computers

We have established that quantum computers are much more powerful and can make faster calculations when compared to conventional computers. Right now, quantum computers are still mostly theoretical and their uses are yet to be determined. There are a few companies and startups like Google and IBM that are currently working on quantum computers. They have quantum computers that are only at 50 qubits. So, for now, the uses for quantum computers are only theoretical and those who are developing them are looking at their other potential uses.

Chemical Models

Because of the sheer amount of processing power, a quantum computer has, it can perform complex calculations and simulate how individual atoms behave. These computations will help develop new materials and substances that we humans use. One of the goals of using quantum computers for chemical models is to simulate ammonia. Ammonia is a key ingredient in the manufacturing of fertilizers. They also hope to find a material that will have superconductive capabilities at room temperature. The current superconductors we have still require extremely low temperatures before they work. This will revolutionize the transportation of goods and people.

Cryptography

Another field where supercomputers can be applied is in cryptography. This field deals with codes, passwords, and encryption. Current computers do have the capability to crack codes and passwords but they take a lot of time. With the help of a supercomputer, the calculations can be done at a fraction of the time currently taken.

The use of quantum computers for this purpose is somewhat like a double-edged sword. While it will help in making security for data much better, with its capabilities, it will also be much easier to crack those defenses.

Business and Finance

A quantum computer can be also be used in the business and finance fields. It can help optimize the flow of resources and products that a company needs or makes. The quantum computer can find the best route, lowest price, and thus, can be used to make more profit. It can also be used to make logistics and scheduling a whole lot easier. Managers and supervisors handle a lot of data every day at work. They may be responsible for inventory, machines, production rate, etc. With the help of a quantum computer, he or she can just input the data and receive relevant information about the task he or she is doing.

Machine Learning

One of the first uses of quantum computers that were seen as possible was in regards to machine learning. Earlier, we have tackled artificial intelligence and how it develops. We also touched upon the goals and dreams of those who create it. In essence, they want to recreate the human brain, or at least its functions, by using artificial materials and processes. As we have established, the work on an AGI may be years or decades—maybe even centuries—away. What the field of AI needs in order to fulfill those dreams is a computer so much more powerful than the ones we have now. And, with a quantum computer, that dream might just become a reality. Quantum computers are vastly more powerful and faster than our current computers so, they may have the speed and power required in order to develop a 'complete' AI program. An AI program can use a quantum computer to search through millions and millions of data in order to improve itself. Again, the development of advanced AI may come with some risks that we have tackled earlier in this book. But one thing is for sure if quantum computers become more abundant and practical, the next thing we see might be a very advanced AI program.

Quantum Computers and the Human Brain

The human brain is the most complicated mechanism we know. It runs our bodily functions while still giving us the power to have ideas, to dream, and to imagine. This very important organ also gives us consciousness and the ability to think. It truly is a powerful machine.

But a lot of people are having an interesting idea. They say that the human brain is, in fact, a quantum computer. We all know that the brain and a conventional computer have a lot of similarities. They both get information from outside itself, convert it into something it can understand, make decisions based on that information, and perform actions in response to that information. And this is essentially how they are similar. A computer and the human brain are similar in process. But some claim that quantum phenomenon like superposition and entanglement also happens in the brain and that the brain can perform advanced calculation in quantum computing. Now, we'll check if the brain is really an organic quantum computer.

Finding the Root of Consciousness

We humans often take things for granted. Well, at least, the general population does. We have a lot of things to think about and worry about. We have to find ways to survive and thrive. Thinking and making decisions are essential in our everyday lives. We cannot go through one day without making at least a dozen decisions. Because of this daily grind, we are often not able to think critically about *why* we are able to think. A lot of philosophers and scientists are trying to find the answer to that question. They all know that every human being on the planet has consciousness or the state of being aware of one's surroundings. But no one has yet found out where this state originates.

Consciousness is a very vague and broad term. It not only denotes the ability to know what's around you. Animals know what is around them but we do not consider them to have consciousness. Consciousness also has to do with learning, emotions, memory, and perception. Philosophers are somewhat aware of what it really is but there are still some things that require more explanations. Right now, the meaning of consciousness is still undefined.

You may be ask, "If we still don't know what consciousness actually is, how can we find its root?" And that is a very good question. And it is also a question that still has no answer. What we do know is that human beings have consciousness. We even take it for granted that we can think and feel and imagine. And since we know that the brain is the organ that holds and controls these concepts, it is most likely somewhere inside the brain's structure—or at least that's what scientists are trying to prove.

Some claim that the brain is able to perform all of its functions because it is a quantum computer. This means that the brain is capable of performing quantum phenomena on a regular basis. Right now, most of the quantum phenomena that scientist re-create take place at very low temperatures. They require nearly absolute zero, or -273 degrees Celsius. So, if the brain is a quantum computer, there must be some structure that allows it to have these phenomena at much higher temperatures. If this is true, this discovery will not only prove that the brain is indeed a quantum computer, but it will also pave the way for us to make our own version of it. It will also revolutionize the way we understand the brain and how it works.

Finding the root of consciousness is not going to be an easy task. It will take a lot of time—it may even be impossible. But some scientists have theorized that the brain as a whole is the root of consciousness, not just a part of it. It is the combination of its functions and actions that make humans aware of their surroundings and have thoughts. But this theory does not explain the fact that there are some people alive today whose brains are damaged or chunks of it have been removed, but are still conscious to what is going on around them.

Will the root of human consciousness ever be found? Right now, we do not know. What we do know is this; humans are the only species on the planet that show consciousness. We are able to think and act upon that thinking. We can feel what is around us and also feel emotions that are part of us. All of these abilities are what we are born with. It is up to us to make the best of them and not waste our lives. We have been given the opportunity and the ability to think, to reason, to make decisions, and to feel, so let us make sure that we are using thoughse abilities to good use. Even if the root of consciousness is never found, we owe it to ourselves to be better than what we were before. We, as a species, must continue to improve and evolve the same way that our inventions and innovations do. If we can improve the things that were invented by man, we can also definitely improve ourselves.

The world we live in is ravaged by a lot of calamities and disasters. Hurricanes and earthquakes make the world a scary place to live in. but humans, in a way have made it a lot worse. Because of our innate curiosity, we may have tipped the delicate balance in this world. Yes, we have become the dominant species on the planet, but at what cost? We have invented a lot of things that have improved the way we live, lengthened our life spans, made communication faster and better, but we are yet to discover the reason why we are so curious and want to know more about the world—and beyond. We are planning and developing a lot of devices that can help us think. Our computers, AI programs, and quantum computers are the tools we have that may help us answer the most fundamental questions of our existence. Being able to clearly define what consciousness is will be a great leap in our advancement. Not only will this discovery change the way we see our brain and its functions, but we will also be able to see ourselves better, and hopefully, understand each other better.

There were times when people who do not have the same skin color as we do were seen as animals, just because they looked different. As we understood better, we came to realize that it is wrong to enslave another human being and it was outlawed through most of the world. If the root of consciousness is discovered, through the use of quantum computers or otherwise, it may most likely solve the biggest problems we face. The problems are not natural disasters or calamities, these are problems brought about by humans. War, greed, crime are just some examples. If we understand the brain better, we may be able to understand each other better.

We are living in a world that is getting smaller and smaller every day. It is very easy to talk to someone on the other side of the globe. But what makes us seem closer may also drive us apart. We tend to focus more on our gadgets and electronic devices than the people around us. Once the root of consciousness is found—if ever—this might change. Once we understand each other better, the whole world will be a much better place to live in.

Is the Brain a Quantum Computer?

Scientists know that the brain functions through the use of 'bioelectric' signals that pass from one neuron to the next. These are interpreted as data and are converted by the brain into thoughts and ideas. As saw stated previously, there is a claim that the human mind is a quantum computer. They say that the brain functions with the use of quantum phenomena such as entanglement and superposition. The idea of the brain being a quantum computer has been around for quite some time. The brain was first understood to be a very powerful computer. This is the way the brain functions in the macroscopic scale. The neurons that make up the brain receive data from the senses and interpret them. But there are some brain functions that are yet to be understood. One of these is where consciousness comes from. We have discussed consciousness and its nature in the previous section. Our consciousness is only one of the concepts that scientists believe are functions of the brain that use quantum mechanics.

They are using computations and calculations based on quantum physics, which works on the subatomic level, to explain where it comes from.

The other functions of the brain that scientists are trying to understand, with the help of concepts in quantum mechanics concerns long-term memory. They are trying to find out how it works and how the brain holds these memories.

There are a few studies and research being performed by the world's best scientists to determine if the brain is a quantum computer. They are dedicating billions of dollars to invest in this search. Through these researches, they might be able to find out if the brain truly is a quantum computer.

Problems and Criticisms

These ongoing research and studies are not without problems and criticisms of course. Some argue that it is impossible to prove that the brain is indeed a quantum computer, or if it is, there is no practical way to prove it. Another issue deals with the ethics of even doing so.

Conceptual

The main problem of postulating that brains are quantum computers is that of consciousness. Since philosophers are still not clear as to the definition and source of consciousness, it is still yet to be fully understood. Some theories about consciousness also do not require quantum effects.

Applying quantum effects to concepts that correlate the brain to a quantum computer poses some problems as well. The concepts of decision making have been related to the same idea as "Schrödinger's cat". The mind's decision-making process may be a form of superposition wherein both the decisions exist at the

same time within the brain but once the decision is made, the brain then breaks that quantum state in order for the observed decision to be made.

Practical

The biggest problem that developers of a quantum computer face are called 'quantum decoherence'.

This is because quantum states are so fragile that any form of disturbance will disrupt them and make them lose their quantum state. The quantum states, as we currently understand them, lose their coherence as they form organs and tissues. Some physicists also calculated that the quantum states decay in sub-picoseconds whereas the brain operates in milliseconds. The brain functions are much too slow for it to be considered as using quantum mechanics. The quantum states also require very low temperatures in order for them not to decay. To maintain temperatures of near absolute zero for long periods of time requires a lot of energy and time which will decay the quantum states even more.

The other problem is that the nerve signals themselves are the reason for decoherence of quantum states. The signals create interference that disturbs the quantum state and decays them. But at the subatomic scales, inside the brain's microtubules, the quantum activity may be seen.

Ethical

Studies for quantum mechanics within the human brain are raising some ethical concerns. In order to determine if the brain uses quantum states in its function, a normal, live human brain is required. This is the biggest roadblock in this study. The limits on the possible experiments and inspection of a human brain make finding these quantum states extremely difficult—almost impossible. Another issue is that some astrologist, paranormal experts, and even some religious leaders are using technical terms used by physicists and are stretching them to mean almost everything they want to.

The use of these phrases incorrectly leads to misunderstanding and muddies the waters for theoretical physics. A lot of influential 'mental healer' is using the terms of quantum mechanics incorrectly and this leads to confusion and misinterpretation with regards to the technical terms.

Quantum Cognition

Concepts within quantum mechanics can be used to find ways to explain some of the brain's processes. This concept is called quantum cognition. This idea does not use quantum mechanics concepts directly to explain the processes in the brain. Instead, it supposes that quantum probability and quantum information theory are more useful in describing these processes.

As was stated earlier, a quantum computer does not try to find the individual information about a specific set of data. It only gives us the correlation or relationship between them that applies to the whole set. The quantum cognition theory applies this principle in the process of decision making. Instead of taking the probability of every action in the decision, the effect of the whole decision is taken into account. "Looking at the big picture" is similar to the idea. The quantum cognition theory states that this is the way the human mind makes its decisions. Quantum probability also applies to the probability or the likelihood of events or situations happening that help humans make judgments. The concept of entanglement has also been hypothesized to be linked to knowledge and memory.

This is the way, as the theory suggests, the brain stores the knowledge and information it receives. This concept is also linked to the way humans retrieve information that is stored in the brain's memory storage.

So, to answer our question if the brain is a quantum computer, in some cases the brain acts like one but in a way we do not know how. Scientists and experts who understand quantum physics and mechanics are still unsure if the brain uses quantum phenomena for its processes, but there is a possibility. So, as far as we know, the brain is not a quantum computer. But it is still up for debate. Maybe in the future, once we understand the inner workings of the human brain a whole lot more, we will know for sure. And the development of more powerful devices and equipment will be vital to this. The development of a quantum computer will not only change the way we live, but it will also change the way we think.

What the Future Holds

The future is an uncertain thing. We do not know what will happen tomorrow. We do not even know what will happen in the next hour. But one thing is for sure, the future is going to arrive, no matter how much we want to stop it. There is nothing short of a miracle that will stop the forward progress of time. So, what can we do? What we, as humans, can do is to move forward as well. There's pretty much nothing else we can do.

But as far as technology is concerned, the future is coming fast. There are things that people fifty years ago never even dreamed possible. If you had a time machine and brought back a person from the early 1900's to the present, he would be baffled. He will most likely be confused and possibly amazed.

Technology is advancing very quickly, especially with the aid of computers. The advent of computers has changed the way we live drastically. Computers have been integrated into almost every aspect of our lives. What will the future be like? How will the lives of people change? If we were to travel forward in time, what would we see?

A lot of people have been trying to predict what the future holds. Movies and science fiction novels are full of stories and ideas of what the future will be like. Flying cars, personal planes, and general purpose robots are only a few examples of these ideas. But, realistically speaking, what can we expect for the future? In the next decades, there will be a lot of advancements in technology. Right now, we are having crises in power and energy. We are using up a lot of energy, but the sources for this energy are very limited. We are still relying heavily on fossil fuels. But most probably in the future, we will be less reliant on them. Not only because they are going to be extremely rare, but we will develop something to replace them entirely. Right now, the biggest competition for fossil fuels as the main source of energy is solar power. But solar panels are expensive and heavy. With advances in technology and materials science, developing cheap and light solar panels will stop us in heavily relying on fossil fuels.

Transportation and cars themselves will be changed. Automated vehicles are becoming more and more efficient— there are just a few kinks to sort out. In the future, driving might not be a necessary skill anymore the same way that horseback riding is right now. Automated vehicles will change the way we move and transport goods and products. The way these cars are powered will also most likely be different. Instead of using gasoline, these cars will most likely be electric. There are a lot of electric cars on the market right now, like the Tesla, but they are still a minority. In the future, this might just be the way we power our cars, whether they are automated or not.

The field of medicine and health care will also be revolutionized. As stated previously, artificial doctors are becoming more and more prevalent and effective.

They can help diagnose patients faster and more accurately than a human doctor can. Robots and automated machines might also be able to perform major surgeries in the future. Not only will that, but the science of prosthetics also change. Not only will the artificial limbs or body parts look like the original, but they may also **feel** like them. This is mainly due to the advancements in AI technology which helps the prosthetic "talk" to the brain and responds like an organic limb. We may also be able to "grow" body parts or at least internal organs. Not like lizards growing back their tails, though. These 'grown' organs are created in a lab and made from actual human cells. This will not only make transplants easier, but it will also make them safer.

We have robots right now. But they are simple ones that only do simple tasks. There are more advanced robots that can do multiple tasks but these are still very expensive and are still very basic. But in the future, every person may have a general purpose robot. These robots can do almost anything. This situation may have both good and bad effects. If these robots are used for good, they will definitely benefit human lives. But we all know their potential as weapons for war. They can be used for other destructive purposes. It is not exactly a robot takeover. It is the use of robots for nefarious deeds that is dangerous. If robots are turned into weapons, they can be sent to do a lot of bad things to people without bringing harm to the people controlling them.

Advancements in computer programming are inevitable. As technology grows so does the language computers use. Not only will computer programs become more complex, but they will also become more powerful. In the future, it might be possible that a 'complete' artificial intelligence is developed.

This will be a great help to human lives if used properly. The development of AGI will change the way we live in ways we cannot yet imagine. This form of AI may become indistinguishable from humans, as far as intelligence is concerned. A superintelligence may even be created that will change the way we see intelligence and can help solve our problems. These machines, of course, can be used for evil purposes. So, if ever they are created, the security and proper use of them should be ensured. The Three Laws of Robotics that the novelist Isaac Asimov made may be the closest approximation of what we need to do in order to remain in control over these creations.

More powerful computers will be available in the future. That is pretty much certain. How powerful? We do not yet know. But the trend in the development of computer technology shows that its growth is exponential. When computers were first developed, they were specialized machines designed to solve very specific problems. They were also very large and took up a lot of room—in some cases a whole room. But as technology and more advanced materials were developed, the computers became faster and more powerful. They began to be commercially available to use for everyone. Not only did they become more powerful, but they also became more compact. Computers nowadays are as normal as telephones were back in the days. Almost every person has at least seen a computer. Most people have one and use it every day. Our smartphones are computers that are very compact and powerful. If you compare the smartphones we have today, they are multiple times much more powerful and faster than the early supercomputers. They can perform calculations at great speeds. Now imagine just how fast and powerful the computers of the future will be like. The development of quantum computers will change the way we live and how we see ourselves. We can use these to develop better materials and substances to improve the lives of every person on the planet.

Not only will that, but the development of quantum computers also help us understand our brain a lot more.

So, if you are looking for what will happen in the future, you have to look back at the developments that have happened in the past. The trends of the past, as far as technology is concerned, will most likely continue. In the future, we will have better materials for our structures and construction. We will also have better ways of transporting goods and services will be changed. The hopes of future studies are bright especially for the improvement of human lives. Advancements in science and technology are going to have bigger impacts on the lives of all people than ever before. Better computers and more advanced technology will bring about a great change in the way humans in the future will live. We humans may change by incorporating and augmenting the technological advancements directly to our bodies. This will improve our own inborn abilities and capabilities and may bring up the abilities we did not even know we had.

The future of the human race is truly very bright!

Conclusion

Humans have always wondered. We are curious creatures and our curiosity seems to be insatiable. We have a tendency to try to know everything and achieve everything. The limits of human curiosity and creativity are yet to be found.

The human brain is a very powerful machine that has taken nature billions of years to create. It uses signals and stimuli from the surroundings to make decisions and ideas based on them. It makes decisions that only take milliseconds from the gathering of information about the stimuli to the reaction of the body. Not only does it control the voluntary actions of the body, but it also controls and regulates the involuntary actions of the body. These functions are essential and vital to the lives of humans like breathing, blood circulation, and digestion. The brain is made up of three major parts: the cerebrum which controls the thoughts, ideas, and emotions; the cerebellum which aids the cerebrum and regulates some of the senses; and the brain stem which is the control center for all the automatic and involuntary functions of the body like breathing, blood circulation, and digestion of food. The human brain is also where the decisions are made and memories of humans are stored.

One of the main goals of computer science is to create an AI, or artificial intelligence, program that is indistinguishable from a human. They aim to recreate the functions of the human brain through the use of only clever computer programming. The three types of AI are weak AI, Strong AI or AGI, and the superintelligence. Weak AI can only do basic tasks. AGI or artificial general intelligence is AI that is indistinguishable from a human intelligence. Superintelligence is the most advanced form of AI that is much more intelligent than a human.

The uses of AI range from transportation and entertainment in the form of games to medical and economics. AI can be used to make our lives easier and they can do the dangerous or dull jobs for us. But they may also be used for evil purposes. AI in itself is not inherently evil. There is nothing evil about the development of it. The biggest problem that the development of advanced AI may bring is that it can replace human workers and there will be a lot of unemployed people.

AI programs may also be used to simulate the way the human brain works. A lot of research is being done to bring AI programs up to the same level as the human brain and intelligence. Although the AI has much more processing power when compared to a human brain, the way it uses its. This is somewhat similar to the idea that is still not like a human brain. Human brains are still more energy efficient and can be used for a multitude of tasks, often at the same time. The next step in computer technology is the quantum computer. Instead of using bits—ones and zeros—a quantum computer uses qubits or quantum bits. These qubits can have a value of one or zero or they can be both at the same time. This makes a quantum computer much more powerful than a conventional computer. It can be used to simulate complicated chemical models. These models can then be used to manufacture more useful materials that we can use to improve our lives. Quantum computers, thanks to their sheer amount of processing power, can be used to create and break codes and passwords. They may be used to keep the most important information and data we have safe and secure from hackers. They can also be used to make financial and business related decisions. They can process a huge amount of data.

They can also be used to improve the infrastructure required for machine learning.

Quantum computers can also be used to understand the human brain a lot better. They can be used to find where consciousness originates. It can also be used to find where the brain stores memories and how the decision-making process is made. But the correlation of the human brain to a quantum computer is largely unproven, as of now. There are no direct ways for scientists and researchers to establish that the brain is a quantum computer. The closest we can try is through the concept of quantum cognition which states that the brain uses quantum probability and quantum information theory to explain how the brain works.

The future for humanity and our technology is very good. Not only will the technology we have become better, but humans themselves may also change. We may become integrated and augmented with our technology to become more than human.

The curiosity of humans to discover our own limits, especially our creativity and ingenuity, is yet to be found. So, these technological advancements will inevitably continue. Where it will take us, nobody knows. But the future is getting brighter every minute.

www.ingramcontent.com/pod-product-compliance
Lightning Source LLC
Chambersburg PA
CBHW061051050326
40690CB00012B/2579